PRAY AS YOU ARE

Finding Your Voice in Prayer

Laura Murray

LUCIDBOOKS

To those who have lost their voice along the way and have the courage to find it again. God is listening.

To my mom, one of the bravest people I know.

CONTENTS

INTRODUCTION

This story has been (partially) husband-approved.

In our first year of marriage, we lived in a small, one-bedroom apartment. One afternoon I was in the bedroom talking (arguing) with God. I was being honest about how I felt and what I thought. I didn't hold back. I rarely did.

Craig and I were raised with different communication styles. His family was more reserved, and my family was the complete opposite. So when I came out of our bedroom to tell Craig about my banter with God, he responded, "You cannot talk to God that way!" (He does not remember saying that, but my memory tells me he did, thus the partial approval of this story.) My response to him was this: "Yes, I can! I have been talking to him like this for my entire life, and if he had a problem with it, he would stop me!" There was not an ounce of doubt in me.

For most of my life I have been honest with God, which has leaned toward wrestling with God. It is in my blood to wrestle. Fast forward 10 years from that first year of marriage. I found myself struggling to talk with God. I was mute. I had spent the past years in various communities that told me how you were and were not supposed to talk to God. Having been silenced and sterilized over the years, I was quieter and more timid, and my honesty had disappeared. What had happened to this wrestler?

Then, in the depths of a painful year of job loss and the demands of a toddler and a newborn, I found my voice again. Pain often makes way for our voice. No more pretend conversations or saying what people thought I should say. No more energy for the façade of sugarcoated prayers. All I had were honest ones. Through suffering and struggles, the wrestler was back, and I slowly stepped back into rich, challenging, and hopeful conversations with God.

Where is your voice in prayer? Have you ever used it? Have you learned there are only certain ways to use it? Where has it been silenced? Where are you longing to speak? Where do you long to pray as you are?

This is exactly where God invites us every day, wherever we are—to pray as we are. The God who created us longs to communicate with us in the everyday, real-deal issues of life. He initiates the conversation repeatedly. The demand of communication is that it is a two-way street; a sender and a receiver are required. He starts, we respond, and this ebb and flow of words, language, passion, silence, pauses, movement, and waiting lead to these rich conversations—prayers that come from places we never knew and lead to the untouched depths of our hearts.

And this is what you will find in the pages of this book: conversations and prayers. There are conversations of those before us who talked face-to-face with the God of the universe—and lived to tell the story. You will find doubters and demanders, the curious and the questioning, the hopeful and the hopeless, the wonderers and the wanderers. You will walk through their stories, read their conversations, and learn about who God is and who you can be before him. You will hear your voice.

My hope and my prayer are that you will find that the God of the universe wants you to be free to converse with him, free to talk, free to listen, free to be. These conversations will reveal to us the freedom we have to pray as we are—to pray as you are. Let your voice be heard. God is listening.

HOW TO USE THIS BOOK

Pray As You Are is a devotional workbook designed to lead you through various spiritual practices, including scripture reading, reflection, and prayer. My desire through this workbook is to help you grow in your relationship with God through growing in conversation with God.

Pray As You Are can be completed on your own or with a small group of people. The chapters are intentionally ordered, but feel free to take each chapter on its own. There are spaces for you to write answers to the practice questions as well as write your prayers.

For each chapter, there are seven parts—one for each day of the week. But you are encouraged to take your time with each chapter, going at the pace the Holy Spirit wants you to go. The days build on each other, so take your time on each one.

You can use any Bible version you prefer with *Pray As You Are*. When specific words are referred to in the devotional studies, they come from the English Standard Version (ESV).

FOR EVERY CHAPTER, YOU WILL FIND THE FOLLOWING:

① An opening prayer
② A short introduction to the topic and story
③ Seven days of devotional and spiritual practices, including the following:
  - Short teachings
  - Scripture readings
  - Practices based on reading for the day
  - Prayers to write based on the reading and practices for the day

OPENING **PRAYER**

Loving God, we begin this study not knowing what we will learn or how we will grow. We begin with anticipation and expectation that you will meet us right where we are. As we enter into your story and our story, help us to see and believe your love, truth, and presence with us. As we express our thoughts honestly, please protect us from any fear or lies that would lead us to want to hide from you. Thank you always for inviting us into conversation and connection with you. Thank you for your grace. Help us to pray as we are. In Jesus's name and by the power of the Holy Spirit. Amen.

CHAPTER ONE

IS IT SAFE?

As a teenager, when I needed money from my dad, I always had a plan. What mood was he in? Was he resting comfortably on the couch, or had he just walked in the door exhausted from work? Where would I find him the most content and happy so when I asked for money, he would say yes? All this analysis went into asking my dad for something I desired, and I made calculations according to the most likely positive outcome.

As I strategized, I also gauged my safety. How safe was it to make this request? Could I truly be honest with the amount of money I needed, or should I hold back in order to get at least a little bit and then ask for more later? Emotionally, I felt nervous. Would my needs be met with rejection or some twenty-dollar bills? What would happen if I was disappointed with his answer? If I did feel disappointed, would I ever have the courage to ask again? Or what if he did give me the money I needed and all my hopes came true?

In risky conversations, we strategize and gauge our safety. We wonder how to start the conversation, what to ask for, and when. We try to assess whether or not we will be heard and, more importantly, understood. We calculate whether it is worth the risk to talk about hard things and to be honest about our thoughts and feelings.

We do the same with God. Is it safe to be honest? Is it safe to ask for what we really want? Is it worth the risk to talk with him about our doubts? Can we really pray as we are?

Conversations (prayers) with God invite us to trust someone we cannot see, to ask without the assurance of specifics, and to hope in God's goodness in a broken world. That's courageous, if you ask me.

GREAT EXPECTATIONS

Starting the conversation is arguably the most difficult part of any conversation with God. We bring many expectations to our prayers. We bring our experiences of rejection and pain from previous prayers. We bring discouragement from times when God was silent. When we are vulnerable enough to ask, we are also vulnerable to disappointment. Whether we are aware of it or not, we bring expectations to our conversations with God, and there is a lot riding on God's response to us.

🏠 **PRACTICE**

Take some time now to consider expectations you have brought into your relationship with God, spoken or unspoken. Think about your family of origin and how your parents or significant people in your life have responded when you expressed your needs. Do you think those somehow influence your expectations of how God will respond?

_____

_____

_____

_____

_____

_____

_____

_____

_____

Next, reflect on the past when you brought certain prayers to God. What did you expect from God? Write down at least one prayer God answered in the way you wanted and another prayer that God did not answer in the way you wanted.

_____

_____

_____

_____

_____

_____

_____

🎙 PRAYER

Spend time in prayer talking to God about your expectations. Ask him to show you how his answers to your prayers have either increased or decreased your confidence that he is truly listening. Ask him to meet you in your disappointments and give you the courage to continue to talk with him in prayer.

_____

_____

_____

_____

_____

_____

_____

_____

THE GIFT OF STORY

To be human is to have stories. Our memories remind us of our own story and the stories of others. Their experiences help shape our stories. As we read the narratives of others and how they interacted with God, we will learn about them, we will learn about God, and we will learn about ourselves. The gift of these stories can fuel our hopes, direct our expectations, and give us the courage to pray as we are.

(m) **PRACTICE**

Use the timeline below to look back on your life and mark:

- Your most significant victories as well as your failures. What did you think about God during those times? Write down your thoughts.
- Any painful times in your life and what those experiences showed you about God. What questions arose as a result?
- Times of clarity and confidence. What did you think about God then?
- Any confusing times. What questions about God surfaced?

_____

_____

_____

_____

_____

_____

_____

🎤 PRAYER

In prayer, take your story to God. Ask him what he wants you to learn and how he desires you to grow. Ask him also to open your eyes, ears, and heart as you read the stories in this book. Write down any other prayers you have for this study.

_____

_____

_____

_____

_____

_____

_____

_____

REPEATED MESSAGES

Outside voices can influence our approach to God. We have been told what we can and cannot say to God as if he only hears certain words—pristine, untainted words with no hint of doubt, sadness, or frustration. We may have been told we must pray in a particular way in order to be heard. We have been told, directly or indirectly, that we can only pray if we are good at it. These voices become repeated messages in our minds, leading us to confinement in prayer. Criticisms lead to doubt and fear.

The truth is that prayer is imperfect, and we will stumble on our words and even say the "wrong" things. God is not waiting for a reason to reject your prayers but longs to hear your heart. God does not expect perfection and performance. He wants you. He knows every quiet longing in your soul, and His grace covers them all. He longs to listen to our musings and our stumblings, our joys and our sorrows. We don't have to be perfect. We never will be.

PRACTICE

Read Psalm 62:8. What are you invited to do? What messages have you believed? What stories replay in your mind, persuading and convincing you that God does not want to hear from you?

Take your time writing the answers to these questions. Include any repeated messages, including any positive ones.

_____

_____

_____

_____

_____

_____

_____

_____

_____

_____

🎙 PRAYER

Take these repeated messages to God in prayer. Ask God one simple thing: "What messages need to be erased and rewritten?" Give God time and space to respond. If something stands out as you listen to him, write it down. Next, ask God, "How do these messages need to be rewritten?" Come back to this prayer as you continue through this book. He will rewrite the messages.

If you don't have anything now, that is okay. Come back and fill in your thoughts later.

_____

_____

_____

_____

_____

_____

_____

_____

REAL LIFE

Let's talk real life. Work, school, noise, community service, family, house management, physical and emotional illness, and more can hinder our prayer life. Our life is cluttered with our to-do lists, even the basics such as eating, showering, home upkeep, and physical health. Where is there time for a conversation?

Having recently come out of the stage of caring for newborns and toddlers, I understand the weariness of the mind and body. Who wants to start a potentially difficult conversation with God when emotional and physical exhaustion have taken their toll? Amid such realities, where do we find the quiet we need for prayer?

PRACTICE

Moment of truth: You must choose to make the time for prayer. Prayer is our lifeline of sanity in a noisy, overwhelming world. It is up to you to schedule the time to pray.

Look at your day and consider all habits that waste time—social media, television, shopping, and more. Write them down. Look at these habits and choose to cut 10 minutes out of one of them. Choose to pray for those 10 minutes. Do more if you would like, but start with 10 minutes.

_____

_____

_____

_____

_____

_____

_____

_____

_____

_____

_____

🎙 PRAYER

Write a prayer expressing the challenges of choosing time to pray. It might be embarrassing to be honest, but honesty is necessary. Ask God to show you how to use your time. Ask God to give you the strength and perseverance to hold onto a time slot to talk with him.

_____

_____

_____

_____

_____

_____

_____

_____

_____

_____

STANDARD PRACTICE

Being creatures of habit, we develop routines in the way we approach God in prayer. We often begin with the same words. Sometimes we start in the same place. We also come with certain perceptions about God and about ourselves. We may even come to God asking Him to meet the same needs, month after month, only to walk away feeling as if our words have fallen on deaf ears. As with any other practice, our prayers are shaped by what we repeat. These thought patterns, whether they are hopeful and expectant or doubtful and apathetic, shape our prayer lives.

PRACTICE

Spend some time reflecting on how you approach prayer. Do you prefer to talk to God in a specific place or at a certain time? Do you repeat the same words? Do you feel the same emotions? What has shaped your prayer life?

_____

_____

_____

_____

_____

_____

_____

_____

_____

_____

Now, ask God to show you his insights on how you come to prayer. Simply say this prayer:

God, would you show me how I come to you in prayer? Show me if I hold back or hesitate. Show me if I pause to listen or nervously do all the talking. Show me whether I come forth honestly, with boldness. Show me where I am afraid. Amen.

Spend a few minutes in silence. Repeat portions of this prayer, if you like.

_____

_____

_____

_____

_____

🎙 PRAYER

Based on your reflections and prayer above, ask God to help you as you continue to grow in confidence and courage in prayer. Write out a prayer to God, asking him to help you grow in the areas above.

_____

_____

_____

_____

_____

_____

_____

_____

_____

GRACE TO GROW

We are so hard on ourselves. We recognize our need to grow; yet in adulthood, we rarely give ourselves the grace to grow. We expect to master new tasks, quickly getting frustrated with ourselves and embarrassed when we cannot perform. We deny ourselves the grace to grow that we desire to show to others. Why are we so hard on ourselves?

🕊 PRACTICE

Pay attention to your reservations about prayer. Do you have high expectations for yourself during this study? How can you give yourself grace to grow as you pursue new goals in your prayer life? How can you allow yourself the freedom to stumble? Read Romans 8:26–27 and reflect on the role of the Holy Spirit in prayer. Write down the ways you can lean on the Holy Spirit as you learn to pray.

_____

_____

_____

_____

_____

_____

_____

_____

_____

_____

_____

_____

🎤 PRAYER

Write a prayer to God, asking for the grace to grow. Write a prayer asking God to help you lean on the Holy Spirit as you learn in this study. Write down any goals you have for yourself in this study and ask the Holy Spirit to give you strength to achieve them.

_____

_____

_____

_____

_____

_____

_____

_____

_____

_____

_____

_____

_____

_____

PRESSURE'S OFF

The pressure is off. God comes to us first. He initiates the conversation and always does. We don't have the first words, but he does. Our Father relentlessly invites us into an ongoing conversation—to talk with him through his word to us in Jesus. And it is because of Jesus we can talk so freely with him. God also provides us with the Holy Spirit to communicate and walk with us.

In prayer, we bring our deepest longings to God. We make space for conversation. But we can only do that because He pursued us first. He moves toward us before we begin to move and make space for him.

PRACTICE

Read John 1. How did God take the initiative? Spend time meditating on John 1. Write down anything that stands out.

_____

_____

_____

_____

_____

_____

_____

_____

_____

_____

_____

_____

_____

_____

_____

🎤 PRAYER

In prayer, express gratitude for God's love, grace, and initiative. Ask him to remind you of the truth of his love and faithfulness. Spend time in prayer enjoying God.

_____

_____

_____

_____

_____

_____

_____

_____

_____

_____

_____

_____

_____

OPENING **PRAYER**

Gracious God, how we want to take you at your word of invitation. We want to respond to your consistent call to come as we are and pray as we are. Yet we have wounds. We have experiences that tell us not to trust anyone and to protect ourselves at all costs. Would you meet us in our doubts? Holy Spirit, would you give us faith to talk with you, believing you for the impossible? May we have the humility and the boldness of Mary, who surrendered to your will and trusted you would fulfill it. She stood firm on your promise of faithfulness. May we trust you and follow you wherever you lead us. We ask these things as Mary did, with curiosity, surrender, and confidence. Amen.

2 | 📖 LUKE 1:26-38

CHAPTER TWO

HOW?

The impossible—we wonder how it will happen. We cannot imagine how it will come to be. How will God provide the income we need? How will our loved one's heart be changed? How will the addiction be abandoned? How will lasting transformation come to the systemic injustices in our broken world? When we cannot imagine how our prayers will be answered, we believe they are impossible.

As a child, I experienced a deep pain that paved the way for 25 years of bitterness. Someone had hurt me, and when I told my mom about it, her response lacked what I longed for—her reassurance and love. I needed her emotional and physical presence, and her vacant response hurt me greatly. As an adult, I learned more about her response and that she never meant to hurt me. No parent is perfect.

The wounds of that emotional and physical absence lingered for years. As the wounds deepened, I chose to keep her at a distance to protect myself from further anguish. I held on to unforgiveness for a quarter of a century. While going through the ordination process to become a pastor, I remember asking my husband Craig, "How can I be a pastor when I have this bitterness in my heart?" It was an integrity issue for me. Yet I had no idea how this deep bitterness would flee.

A few months later I prayed, "God, I don't care. I don't care about my relationship with my mom. I don't care if I stay in bitterness. But if you care, you do something about it. Amen." That was it—honest, plain, and hardly a pastoral prayer. I didn't care if God moved, let alone how he would move. A couple months later, my mom came to my house on one of her regular visits to see our kids, her only grandchildren. I remember waking up that morning, and the bitterness was gone. Gone! There was no fire to be fueled, no bitterness and unforgiveness, just release and freedom. The embers that stayed lit, ready to explode into flames at the sight, voice, or touch of my mom, were snuffed out. It was so strange and so true at the same time. I didn't know what to do. I even tried to stoke the embers, not believing they were truly extinguished. Nothing happened. By God's great grace, he gave me the gift of forgiveness. He gave me the gift of release from bitterness. I cannot explain how he did it; I just know that he did.

And that is often how God responds to our how questions. He simply does whatever he promises to do. These huge, unimaginable promises are fulfilled. And we can hold him to his promises.

God is with us in our impossibilities, inviting us to talk to him about them. He wants to hear everything from us. Yet it is not necessarily about the impossible being made possible, but about God himself. Do we trust him? Do we believe he will do what he says he will? Can we take him at his word? Throughout the Bible, God makes promises to us, and he tells us he will keep them. He cannot deny himself. Do we believe that?

Sometimes, it takes us a while to believe. It took me 25 years.

Mary, the mother of Jesus, asked the how question. She had her questions and curiosities about how this whole virgin birth thing would work. And what we find in Mary is a surrender of trust and a gutsy move to believe that God would keep his word.

WHEN WORDS TROUBLE

Surprising words can leave us speechless, confused, and unsure about how to respond. Whether it is the announcement of a birth or a loss, a life-altering diagnosis or a life-giving medicine, the unexpected often takes our breath—and our words—away. So many things are happening within us in that moment—thoughts and images, emotions and adrenaline. Troubling words demand change. And when we pay attention to God's words, his words change us.

Gabriel, an angel of God, approached Mary with troubling words. As she received them, she tried desperately to make sense of them. The whys and hows of Gabriel's announcement bewildered Mary.

⌂ PRACTICE

Read Luke 1:26–29. The writer, Luke, sets up the story, describing who Mary was and where Gabriel came from. God sent an angel to speak to a human being. Write down the ways Mary responded. Notice the words used to describe Mary's feelings and what was going on in her heart.

_____

_____

_____

_____

_____

_____

_____

_____

Consider a time when God's words spoke to you and you were left feeling and thinking like Mary—perplexed, curious, anxious to figure things out. What was that like?

_____

_____

_____

_____

_____

_____

_____

🎙 PRAYER

Whether through scripture, the words of a friend, a prayer, or the Holy Spirit, we hear God's words but don't know what he means. Take some time to consider some of God's words to you that have you stumped. Then write a prayer, asking God to meet you where you are, stumped within your thoughts, feelings, and attempts at understanding.

_____

_____

_____

_____

_____

_____

_____

_____

WHEN WORDS COMFORT

When faced with the unknown, fear often overtakes our thoughts. Our imaginations go into full gear as we think of limitless scenarios of our future and try to picture what is to come. Fortunately, God is prepared for that. Just as God's words can surprise us, they can also encourage us.

Before Mary could get a word out, Gabriel spoke again, telling her of God's love and favor. He knew what she needed before she said a word.

(i) PRACTICE

Read Luke 1:30. As you read this verse, picture how these words might have made Mary feel in that moment. Have you ever had someone speak a word before you knew you needed it? What did that do to your feelings and thoughts? Think about your emotions and feelings at that time. Write them down.

_____

_____

_____

_____

_____

_____

_____

_____

_____

_____

_____

_____

🎤 PRAYER

God is ready to speak to us before we even know we need his words of reassurance. Today, set a timer for 10 minutes and sit in silence for the full 10 minutes. Ask God to speak to you about what you need to hear. If you get distracted, focus on the truth that God sees you. Write down the words of encouragement, trust, and reassurance you sense from God.

_____

_____

_____

_____

_____

_____

_____

_____

_____

_____

_____

_____

_____

DEMAND TO KNOW

Information is helpful. It gives us understanding and helps us think and take the next steps. The only risk in asking for more information is that you might get more than you wanted. We have access to so much information that we have learned to rely on it to great lengths. With God, we demand information, and God does not always allow us to know. Yet even if he elects to withhold details, we are still welcomed to ask, "How?"

Gabriel spoke surprising news to Mary. Whoa! Wait a minute. What? Bomb drop—you are going to give birth to a son. Here is your son's name, and by the way, he will rule the world. Right, got it!

Mary's response to Gabriel's life-changing announcement was something like this: "Give me the facts, sir. In case you didn't notice, I am a virgin and these things don't happen to virgins."

Mary asked, "How?"

(i) PRACTICE

Read Luke 1:31–34. Notice the tone of the conversation between Gabriel and Mary. In addition to her words, what do you notice about Mary's attitude?

How do you respond to outrageous news? How is your attitude? Do you sit quietly, contemplating? Do you ask a deluge of questions? Do you deflect and change the subject? Do you remain skeptical without proof? What can you learn from Mary's response in the story?

_____

_____

_____

_____

_____

_____

_____

_____

🎙 PRAYER

Is there something in your life you avoid asking God about? Is there a step of faith he wants you to take? Is "how?" part of the conversation that needs to happen? In your prayer today, mimic Mary's question and fill in your own words where Mary's are underlined. "How <u>will this be</u>, since <u>I am a virgin</u>?" Take this question to God in prayer.

_____

_____

_____

_____

_____

_____

_____

_____

_____

_____

ANYTHING BUT ORDINARY

Some of our hows come with simple answers, and many do not. How will the issue be solved? How will we now live? How will my family have enough? How will we continue without this person? How will this new life change us? Sometimes, the answers to these questions stretch our comprehension and our faith. The answers provided might be clear but not so simple.

Gabriel pushed Mary beyond her human imagination, just as God continues to push beyond ours today. Gabriel was straightforward and clear in his answer, yet the content of his answer was mind-blowing, something like this: "The Holy Spirit will create a new life within you, Mary." Skip basic biology and the birds and the bees. This new life in Mary's womb would be wholly different than every other baby.

🏠 PRACTICE

Read Luke 1:35. Reflect on the words from Gabriel and the matter-of-fact feel to them. Have you received information that caused you to have even more questions? What do you do when your pursuit of information does not satisfy your curiosity or does not provide the answer you prefer? Do you continue to seek other answers? Do you give up? Has God ever given you an answer that is clear yet far from simple?

_____

_____

_____

_____

_____

_____

_____

_____

_____

_____

_____

🎤 PRAYER

As God listens to our questions and curiosities, he responds in various ways. At times, he gives us information and insight. At other times, he responds with quietness and silence. Look back at your responses in the above practice. Talk to God in prayer about how and why you pursue and demand answers. Ask him to show you what is at the core of your pursuit of information.

_____

_____

_____

_____

_____

_____

_____

_____

_____

_____

_____

_____

_____

PICTURES OF THE POSSIBLE

When walking through an impossibility, it helps to know we are not alone. In addition to the empathy of someone else's story, we also need the hope of their story. We need stories of the impossible made possible—God's miracles working their way through the stories of others. Our faith needs these stories.

Gabriel reminded Mary of the story of her barren cousin, Elizabeth, who was six months pregnant. Elizabeth's pregnancy story was completely different than Mary's. Who knows how often Elizabeth and her husband, Zechariah, had tried to get pregnant to no avail? But Elizabeth's miraculous pregnancy became part of Mary's story. God provided encouragement to Mary as Gabriel shared the story of the impossible made possible in Elizabeth's life.

⌂ PRACTICE

Read Luke 1:36–37. When has the story of someone else's impossible situation made possible encouraged you to believe God for the impossible? Write their story and yours.

_____

_____

_____

_____

_____

_____

_____

_____

_____

_____

_____

_____

_____

🎙 PRAYER

Write a prayer to God, thanking him for the stories of the impossible made possible. Also, express any disappointment in his slowness to act or any discouragements in your impossible situation. Make a choice to thank God for his goodness, his power, and his love. Ask him for more pictures of his goodness, power, and love while you ask how.

_____

_____

_____

_____

_____

_____

_____

_____

_____

_____

_____

LIVING FAITH

When we put our minds to it, we can accomplish anything, right? We often foolishly believe that life depends on us. We credit ourselves with having more power than we actually do. If we have enough money, we can solve our family problems. If we have the right opportunities and connections, we can achieve success. If we dream it, we can have it.

Yet many things happen to us rather than because of us. We may have been born into wealth and physical giftedness. We may have received special opportunities for education or unique privileges. Mixed in with these variables could be a family history of addiction, a special needs child, an unfaithful spouse, the sin consequences of others, and on and on. Whether or not we will admit it, most of the variables in our lives are beyond our control.

In the midst of life's uncontrollable variables, God announced Mary's pregnancy. Mary never asked and she never did anything to receive this call in life. And her response was as unfathomable as the story itself.

🕯 PRACTICE

Read Luke 1:38. What is Mary's simple response? What does she consider herself? And what does this posture lead her to do?

What posture do you take when you think about God? Do you take a posture similar to Mary's, or do you expect God to be your servant, serving your dreams and ambitions? How does Mary's response encourage you to reconsider your posture toward God and what he asks of you?

_____

_____

_____

_____

_____

_____

_____

_____

_____

_____

_____

🎙 PRAYER

Talk to God about the times you have asked how and been dissatisfied with his answer. Be honest with your posture toward God. Talk to him about any struggles to surrender to what he wants you to do. Allow him to meet you as you are. Take your time in prayer, and then ask him to form in you a posture of surrender, as he did in Mary.

_____

_____

_____

_____

_____

_____

_____

_____

CHAMPIONING OUR CALL

When we play the comparison game with others, we lose sight of God's call. Whether it is success or a stage of life, opportunities or lack of movement, we often look at those around us, gauging their value and ours. How often do we compare our lives with theirs? He has created each of us with unique callings, and our greatest satisfaction is found when we fulfill his call for our lives.

Mary and Elizabeth had two similar yet different calls. As one's disgrace was taken away through a pregnancy, another was given disgrace as she became pregnant as a virgin. Yet they both celebrated one another and the goodness of God as he called them to do a special work. This work from God was not about them but about God, his power, and his faithfulness. When God called them, Mary and Elizabeth responded as his humble servants. These women knew that God loved them, and they loved him in return. What these women literally and spiritually carried was ultimately for the sake of others.

In the midst of her asking how, God gave Mary more than answers; he gave her a friend. Elizabeth was someone to celebrate with, to provide encouragement, and to walk with Mary in this call to carry and raise the Son of God.

🕌 PRACTICE

Read Luke 1:5–7, 24–25, 39–45. As you read portions of each woman's story, consider that Elizabeth championed Mary's call. Do you have someone in your life who provides encouragement as you follow God? This week, tell them thank you. Is there someone in your life you can champion? Is there someone you can walk with as they live out their call? Write down ideas of who these people might be.

_____

_____

_____

_____

_____

_____

_____

_____

_____

_____

_____

🎤 PRAYER

Spend time writing a prayer for anyone you listed above. Ask God whether he wants you to do anything more than pray for them, and then step out in courage to do so. At the very least, share your prayer with them as a word of encouragement.

_____

_____

_____

_____

_____

_____

_____

_____

OPENING **PRAYER**

Gracious God, we don't know why you ask certain people to carry certain burdens. Really, you don't even ask; they just have to carry them. And these burdens get so heavy. God, we pray for those carrying heavy loads. We pray for those carrying new burdens. We pray for those who watch while loved ones carry loads they cannot share. In your goodness, give them strength, courage, hope, and joy as they carry these heavy weights. Would you remind them that Jesus is with them and that he understands? Would you enable us to love them well and help carry their burdens? Please lighten their loads, even if for just a moment. We pray these things in Jesus's strong name. Amen.

CHAPTER THREE

TAKE THIS

My younger sister Annie has Down syndrome. I don't know why she has to carry this load, but she does. I have asked God this question many times. I have wondered what it is like to carry it. I have imagined what life would be like if it were taken away. Will it be taken away in heaven when all things are good and right? Or will parts of the load be part of her story and part of her being made whole? I wonder.

I also wonder what it is like for so many others who carry lifelong burdens. Why is someone born into an abusive family? Why is someone born with a genetic disposition to addiction? Why is someone born in a country where their worth is less than property? I grieve with those who carry new and unexpected loads. Why can they no longer walk? Why is their loved one so sick? Why is their memory failing?

I have been asked to carry a load from childhood. Even though much healing has come, I still carry some consequences from it like doubt, fear, and deep mistrust. I hate that I have to carry this load—a load that was the result of someone else's sin. I live in hope that one day I will no longer have to bear this heavy weight, but my release may not come until heaven.

We don't want to trudge through life with these loads weighing us down. We don't want these loads for our loved ones, for our friends, and for even a stranger. Some of these are burdens we would not wish on our worst enemies. They come as a consequence of this broken and sin-filled world. We did not ask for this brokenness, and yet it found us. It finds all of us. And under the weight of these loads, we can dare to ask God to take them away.

Jesus dared to ask. He asked God three times to take away a load—a load that was the result of sin and brokenness and a load that led to his death. He asked, and God never took it away.

YOUR LOAD

Loads are heavy, and burdens wear us out. We want to be free from our loads, but we are not. We live with these realities. We all have loads and burdens we carry. What is your burden? What has God asked you to carry? Have you asked God to take it away and yet it remains?

Jesus, the Son of God, was given a great load to carry. He was the only one who could carry it. He understands what it feels like to shoulder a heavy load.

🏠 **PRACTICE**

Read Matthew 26:36–46. Read this story two or three times, slowly. Sit in the story. Are there words or phrases that stand out or cause you to pause? Write these down.

Now sit in your story. What loads do you have? What is weighing you down?

Give yourself time to listen to what God wants to say to you through Jesus's story. Take time to imagine yourself doing the things Jesus did. Be honest with yourself regarding your thoughts and feelings. Write down anything God brings up.

_____

_____

_____

_____

_____

_____

_____

_____

_____

_____

_____

_____

🎙 PRAYER

Practice praying in quiet for 15 minutes. Use as few words as possible. Simply meditate on Jesus's story and the words and phrases you wrote above. Reflect on what God is showing you through Jesus's story. Allow God to speak to your heart in this silent prayer.

_____

_____

_____

_____

_____

_____

_____

_____

_____

_____

_____

SHARING THE LOAD

No one lives life without carrying loads. Some are obvious, and others are hidden. Each load has a unique depth, length, weight, and cost. No one else can completely understand your burden. And at the same time, our burdens unite us since no one escapes carrying burdens. We all carry loads. We are not alone.

In the garden of Gethsemane, Jesus was not alone. He had friends and asked them to help carry the load by keeping awake, watching, and praying. He asked his friends to stay nearby. Jesus gives us a glimpse of his humanity as he asked his friends to help him.

(icon) **PRACTICE**

Read Matthew 26:36–38. Reflect on Jesus's humanity and the request for his friends' help. Write down the aspects of Jesus's humanity that make an impression on you.

What is it like asking someone to share your load? Do you ask, or do you try to take care of everything yourself? With which friends can you express your deepest thoughts and feelings? Do you believe you can share those with God?

_____

_____

_____

_____

_____

_____

_____

🎤 PRAYER

Talk to God about whether you are comfortable sharing your burdens. Be honest about any fears or issues about how sharing would look. Talk to him about the struggles you have sharing your burdens with another. Spend time asking God to show you the people you can open up to, and ask God to prepare their hearts to share your burden. Write your prayer.

_____

_____

_____

_____

_____

_____

_____

_____

_____

_____

OUR HONESTY

In our desire to be honest, sometimes we compare our burdens to others, leading to feelings of guilt. We may think, "Well at least I don't have it as bad as she does. Maybe I shouldn't struggle so much with my small load." We invalidate our feelings and unique struggles when we compare ourselves. What if we talked to God about our situation and allowed him to meet us and speak to us in our situation? What if we expressed our true desires with our Father without any guilt? Is that possible?

Jesus asked his Father if it were at all possible to take away his load, his cup. Jesus, who jointly created all things with his Father, knew God could have taken away his load. God chose not to, because only Jesus could do this job. In expressing his real desire for this load to be lifted, Jesus modeled for us complete honesty and humble authenticity with his Father.

PRACTICE

Read Matthew 26:39. How does Jesus's honesty encourage you to be honest before God? How does his example empower you to be honest with God about the load you carry?

_____

_____

_____

_____

_____

_____

🎤 PRAYER

Write a prayer to God about your load. In moments when you feel overwhelmed by the weight of your burdens, say with Jesus: *Father, if it is possible, take this cup (name your load) from me.* In silence, allow God to meet you in your honesty and vulnerability.

OUR POSTURE

Humility is learned, and humility is chosen. We learn humility through honesty, recognizing that so much of life is out of our hands. We also choose humility as we take a posture of submission, recognizing our limited power and knowledge and God's perfect power and knowledge.

Jesus demonstrated and lived uncompromising honesty and perfect humility. He had no feelings of guilt as he cried out to his Father. Jesus displayed both honesty and humility before his Father, even though he had access to unlimited power and knowledge. Jesus could have called down angels from heaven to save him. He had power, but he chose not to use it. He chose a posture of humility and surrender, trusting his Father's will.

⟨⟩ **PRACTICE**

Read Matthew 26:39. Read this verse again and consider the posture of humility that Jesus took. What does it look like to be both honest and humble, expressing to God exactly what you desire with hands open to whatever he brings? Do you believe honesty and humility are mutually exclusive? How can you engage both of these attitudes in your prayer life?

_____

_____

_____

_____

_____

_____

_____

_____

_____

_____

_____

_____

_____

🎤 PRAYER

If you are ready, write out a prayer of surrender. If you are not ready, talk to God about why. It's okay. It takes time to surrender. God knows that. Write an honest prayer expressing exactly where you are in the process of surrender.

_____

_____

_____

_____

_____

_____

_____

_____

_____

_____

_____

_____

DISAPPOINTMENTS

In vulnerability, we share the load, and sometimes we are let down. We have the courage to ask for help, and people fail to act. They mean well, but their actions don't back up their sentiments. That hurts! And it opens the door to doubt and skepticism and makes it hard to trust people again. What if they let me down again? Why not protect myself and just not share with anyone? It is already hard to carry the load, so why add disappointment?

Jesus experienced disappointment in his friends. He asked them to stay awake, watch, and pray with him. That is all he asked. But they slept, ignoring the realities he was facing.

🕯 PRACTICE

Read Matthew 26:40–41. Read these verses from Jesus's story and reflect on Jesus's experience of disappointments. What disappointments come up for you? Have these disappointments changed your expectation of people? Do you try again as Jesus did, or do you hold back, afraid of more pain? How do you respond when people say they are there for you but fall asleep instead?

_____

_____

_____

_____

_____

_____

_____

_____

_____

_____

_____

_____

_____

_____

🎙 PRAYER

Bring these pains and disappointments to God in prayer. Express your frustration, anger, sadness, and any other emotion. Write out your prayer and ask him to meet you and heal you so you can have the wisdom and courage to trust again.

_____

_____

_____

_____

_____

_____

_____

_____

_____

_____

_____

_____

_____

ON REPEAT

It is hard enough to share honestly with God without feeling like we are complaining. But what if we pray honestly about the same needs over and over again? If we repeat ourselves, how will God respond? Will he change his answer? Or will he get tired of our persistence?

This was not a one-and-done conversation for Jesus. He asked God to take away his cup three times. Honesty and humility again, and again, and again. There is no indication from the text that God said anything. Jesus expressed his innermost thoughts and feelings and was met with deafening silence.

PRACTICE

Read Matthew 26:36–45. What do you make of Jesus repeating his prayer? Do you get tired of repeating yourself? What have your experiences with God been like? Has he been silent, or has he spoken? Write about your experiences with repeated prayers. How does Jesus's story encourage you?

_____

_____

_____

_____

_____

_____

_____

_____

_____

_____

_____

_____

_____

🎙 PRAYER

Rest in this prayer and repeat it as necessary:

Almighty God, some days are harder than others. I don't want my repetition to seem like I am whining or complaining. It is simply a repeated cry of weariness and hopelessness. I am tired. The future is foggy, and it looks exhausting. Meet me with your grace and overwhelm me with your love, reminding me that you are with me and you hear me. Thank you. Amen.

Add any additional prayers below.

_____

_____

_____

_____

_____

_____

_____

_____

_____

_____

_____

SURRENDER

When do our "Take this away, God!" prayers end? When can we stop repeating and let it go? This place of final surrender—how do we get there? We get there through God's grace and our honesty and humility. This place is different for everyone and unique to each situation. Surrender is more of an art than a science.

Jesus stopped asking and moved forward. We don't know how he knew to move forward, yet he did. We can, too.

🕯 PRACTICE

Read Matthew 26:46. Jesus repeated His request three times, and then he stopped asking and moved forward. Moving on, however, may not be so clear-cut in our lives. When Jesus decided to move forward, he did so with a resoluteness to carry his load and a joy in the purpose to which God had called him. As you reflect on his courage and consider your load, is it time to move forward? How can you move forward with a surrender like Jesus had, with his strength and his joy?

_____

_____

_____

_____

_____

_____

_____

_____

_____

_____

_____

_____

🎙 PRAYER

Write a prayer, asking the Holy Spirit to give you strength, joy, and peace beyond measure. Ask him to give you more than you can imagine as you surrender and go forward to love and live for him so others might know our incredible God.

_____

_____

_____

_____

_____

_____

_____

_____

_____

_____

_____

_____

OPENING **PRAYER**

Holy Father, how you long to make us whole. In your perfection, we find ourselves lacking. In your beauty, we find ourselves longing. We long to be made new, we long for our sin to cease, and we long to bring glory to you. These longings demand our confessions. May we be courageous to confess the ways we have gone against your beauty, your goodness, and your love. Thank you that you promise to meet us with your grace through Jesus. You meet us, cleanse us, and call us to your good works in this world. May we listen, ready to do whatever you ask. In Jesus's gracious name and power. Amen.

CHAPTER FOUR

CLEAN ME

In the summer of 2001, the small college town of Freiburg, Germany, hosted a local performance of Mozart's *Requiem*. The old church held a full orchestra and pews filled with eager listeners. Surrounded by the space of tech-free, perfect acoustics, the music reverberated off the walls and into our souls. We sat in this place of worship, absorbing the movement of sound and the beauty of overlapping notes and instruments. At one point, I had to close my eyes and let the music wash over me. Yet it did more than wash over me; it went in me and stayed there. Its staying power led me to remain speechless after the concert, so much so that a friend was concerned about my silence. I was intoxicated by the beauty of the music, and I wanted it to last forever. One spoken word would break the beauty of it all.

Beauty begets beauty. Beauty moves into our souls and resides there, moving us to create, extend, and expand ourselves.

As the prophet Isaiah stood before God, he was wrapped up in the beauty of worship. He watched the worship of a holy God as magnificent creatures declaring his worth shook the very foundations of that space. As Isaiah got wrapped up in worship, he was changed. Isaiah lingered before a holy God in worship, and then he was drawn into God's presence. Isaiah's worship included confession and prayer, surrender and obedience to God's call.

As beauty draws us in, we also linger before a holy God, wrapped up in his beauty and glory. His beauty changes us. Often, we only get a glimpse of God's beauty. We could not handle more than a taste. These simple and holy glimpses compel us to stop, look, and linger. Sometimes these glimpses are given to us after we have put in an effort to see them, and sometimes they are surprises of grace. They come in a variety of forms. As we give space to God, these glimpses of beauty change us. In our lingering, we are reminded that God is so very different from us, and we find ourselves bowing before him in humble confession. But we do not remain there. God meets us with his cleansing grace and the call to join him in his redeeming work in the world.

HOLY SURROUNDINGS

"You had to be there." People often use that phrase after an incredible experience or even a funny joke. You had to be in that space, in that place, at that time, with those people. The moment cannot be re-created—you had to be there.

Wrapping our minds around Isaiah's experience is quite the challenge. Isaiah had a vision of God, the King, sitting and filling an entire place of worship with his presence. Then, Isaiah saw curious creatures flying before God's throne, calling out to one another, proclaiming God's glory in worship. Back and forth, back and forth, "Holy, holy, holy is the LORD of hosts; the whole earth is full of his glory!" (Isa. 1:3). The sights, smells, and sounds of worship inundated Isaiah and shook the temple's foundations. In this place, Isaiah heard God's voice call him.

🕍 **PRACTICE**

Read Isaiah 6:1–4. Reflect on Isaiah's vision. Close your eyes and imagine the sights, smells, sounds, and space of Isaiah's encounter with heavenly worship. What strikes you as you enter into this imagined space? How do you feel? Are you numb to it? Skeptical of it? Do you long to stand in God's presence with Isaiah and take it all in? Or would you prefer to run? Write down your response to these holy surroundings.

_____

_____

_____

_____

_____

_____

_____

_____

_____

_____

_____

_____

🎙 PRAYER

Practice this simple prayer today: "Holy, holy, holy is the Lord of hosts; the whole earth is full of his glory!" Repeat the prayer slowly a few times. Sit in silence, soaking in the words you read and the holy surroundings you imagined. This time of prayer can be as long as you want as you linger in God's holiness. Add additional prayers of praise to God if you like.

_____

_____

_____

_____

_____

_____

_____

_____

_____

_____

_____

LINGER

Surrounded by the grandness of God reminds us of our humanity, our limits, and our smallness. Again, getting our heads around God seems like a futile effort. Yet the practice of lingering in his greatness develops in us a humble perspective of who we are and who he is.

Yet sometimes we don't stop to linger. Why? Success, achievement, and productivity compel us to move. Our culture pushes us to go farther, faster. To slow down for the deeper moments will impede our success as others pass us by. We have been conditioned to stay on the surface, to keep going, no matter the cost. Depth is not valued, and it is not easy. With this double whammy, it is easy to ignore the call to linger. So we keep moving past these glorious moments where depth calls to us to slow down and shallow progress calls us to move.

Isaiah did not move. Isaiah did not run from this experience or consider it a check mark on his to-do list for the day. Isaiah lingered, he absorbed, he listened, he heard God's voice, and he remained—ready to respond.

⌂ PRACTICE

Read Isaiah 6:1–4. Do you find yourself dodging deeper thoughts and feelings? How have you avoided and ignored the call for depth through worship? How are you tempted to treat worship as a box to check on your to-do list? As you reflect on this, write down your answers.

_____

_____

_____

_____

_____

_____

_____

_____

_____

_____

_____

_____

🎤 PRAYER

Anything you wrote down, take to God in prayer. Be honest and open before God. Write down your prayer, whether it is a confession, a plea for help, or an acknowledgment that today you are just going through the motions of life. Wherever you are in your posture of worship, talk to God about it today.

_____

_____

_____

_____

_____

_____

_____

_____

_____

_____

THE GUEST OF SHAME

At any opportunity, shame comes knocking. Shame is the persistent guest, for in confession, there is opportunity to beat ourselves up. Yet this opportunity is not an invitation from our holy God. He never leads the way to shame. The worship of God leads to conviction, confession, and grace. Through honest confession and the reminder of God's grace, we receive wholeness and healing.

Isaiah's confession is true and honestly spoken before God. There is no shame in confession. Shame has no place in God's grace.

🏛 PRACTICE

Read Isaiah 6:5. When you practice confession, what do you hear? Do you hear a verbal attack in your mind? Do certain words or feelings assault you again and again?

Practice replacing those words with the truth that God never leads the way to shame and that there is freedom and love in the assurance of God's forgiveness and grace.

_____

_____

_____

_____

_____

_____

_____

_____

_____

_____

_____

_____

_____

_____

🎙 PRAYER

Spend time in prayer talking to God about any shame or attacks that happen when you confess. Ask him to free you from these attacks that you might be free to receive his grace and forgiveness.

_____

_____

_____

_____

_____

_____

_____

_____

_____

_____

_____

CONFESSION

Confession takes time. It takes time to reflect and notice the ways we have sinned. Many of us have not experienced a powerful worship experience like Isaiah did, an experience that leads us to confession. When we make the choice to spend time before God in worship, we acknowledge his holiness and our limited humanity. In these times, his ways and our ways become clearer, and we recognize the ways we have not followed him.

In God's presence, Isaiah came face-to-face with his sinful condition. Isaiah confessed his unclean lips and the unclean lips of the people he lived among. Isaiah spoke a very specific prayer of confession, recognizing that no one has the hope of forgiveness apart from the goodness and grace of God.

PRACTICE

Read Isaiah 6:5 again. It takes time to get specific with our confessions. Take 10 to 15 minutes today and consider the greatness of God. Consider his goodness, his perfection, his creativity, and maybe even picture again what Isaiah experienced in verses 1–4. Ask God to remind you of anything you need to confess. Write down any sins you need to confess to God.

_____

_____

_____

_____

_____

_____

_____

_____

_____

_____

_____

_____

🎤 PRAYER

Spend time today in specific confession. As you do, remember there is no shame in confession or in receiving God's grace and forgiveness. We all need it. If there is a confession you are afraid to share with him, tell him about your fears. Ask him to help you trust him. Express the desire for freedom from this sin. Write down these prayers, reminding yourself of God's love, grace, and assurance of forgiveness through Jesus.

_____

_____

_____

_____

_____

_____

_____

_____

_____

_____

CLEANSING

As we have the courage to confess, we sometimes feel the need to make up for it with some type of penance or good works. But God's grace and forgiveness is a free gift. We do not pay to receive it, and we do not owe him anything after it. Our confession is our surrender to God to meet us and cleanse us.

At the sound of Isaiah's confession, a heavenly creature who had been echoing God's praises flew from the altar with a tool of cleansing. This creature, so near to the Lord, moved toward Isaiah.

🕯 PRACTICE

Read Isaiah 6:6–7. Consider Isaiah's movement after he confesses. Notice the movement of the seraphim. Isaiah simply received the cleansing the seraphim brought.

How are you tempted to add to God's forgiveness? Do you feel like you owe him something after he has given you the gift of cleansing? Ask him to show you whether you are adding anything to the no-strings-attached gift of forgiveness.

_____

_____

_____

_____

_____

_____

_____

_____

_____

_____

_____

🎙 PRAYER

Sit in prayerful silence today, allowing the prayer below to work its way into you. In quiet, listen for the goodness and truth God wants to speak to you.

Gracious God, your word says that you love me unconditionally, yet so often I think I owe you something in return for your grace. I want to receive your unconditional love with no strings attached. Help me to believe your great love for me. Help me to live in your grace. Amen.

_____

_____

_____

_____

_____

_____

_____

_____

_____

_____

_____

_____

_____

CLEARING THE WAY

Competing voices surround us, threatening to drown out God's voice. These competing voices often distract us, blur our focus, and combat our pursuit of God. And in the clamor of so much noise, we want to hear God's voice. Confession and cleansing quiet the dissonance so we can hear God's voice. In confession we come honestly; in cleansing we receive freely; and in listening we hear openly. And as the Lord meets us in our places of deepest cleansing, we can listen for his voice and his calling for our lives.

Isaiah sat in worship, confessed, received, and then heard the voice of the Lord openly. And when he heard it, he was ready to engage.

(icon) **PRACTICE**

Read Isaiah 6:8. As you read about Isaiah's recognition of the Lord's voice and his enthusiastic response, to what are you drawn? What in this verse causes you to pause? Is there a particular word, phrase, or action on which God wants you to meditate?

_____

_____

_____

_____

_____

_____

_____

_____

_____

_____

_____

🎙 PRAYER

As God highlights an aspect of this verse to you, bring it to him in prayer. If you have questions, ask him. If you have longings, express them. When it comes to this verse and your life, what do you want to say to God? Spend a few minutes in silence, asking God to speak and echo his truth to your heart. Pay attention to any stirrings or repetitions of his truth and love. Listen for his voice.

_____

_____

_____

_____

_____

_____

_____

_____

_____

_____

CALLING

Isaiah's worship, confession, and cleansing prepared him to receive God's calling for his life. As we worship, confess, and are cleansed, we hear God's call for our lives. These calls are unique and varied, simple and complex, challenging and compelling. Our calls are gifts we offer to this world. And the confidence, courage, and power we are given to fulfill these calls come from God.

Regardless of our calling in life, the fact that it comes from God makes our calling good. God's calling is propelled by his love. The work to which the Lord calls us is empowered by his goodness and his grace.

Isaiah's call was not easy or fun. But the fact that Isaiah heard God gave him confidence to accomplish the work God had for him. God will empower and equip us to fulfill our calling.

🏮 PRACTICE

Read Isaiah 6:1–8. What do you expect the call of Isaiah to be like?

_____

_____

_____

_____

_____

_____

_____

Read Isaiah 6:9–13. As you read Isaiah's call in these verses, what thoughts go through your mind? Are you surprised or confused? If so, why? Write down your expectations of Isaiah's call and the reality of his call.

_____

_____

_____

_____

_____

_____

_____

🎙 PRAYER

Without knowing it, we have expectations we bring to God. We do all the things he asks, and we expect certain things in return. Spend your prayer time talking to God about your expectations. Share with him any disappointments. Ask him to continue to free you to receive the work—the calling—he has for you and to trust him in it. Ask him to help you walk in faith as he calls you to the good works he has for you.

_____

_____

_____

_____

_____

_____

_____

OPENING **PRAYER**

Father God, you give good gifts. The greatest of these gifts is life. You are the breath in our lungs, the air we breathe, and the strength of our song. You never cease to write stories of new life. Even as we say these things, we sometimes wonder why you don't give certain good gifts. We wonder why you allow sickness and death. We wonder why you don't stop violence and evil. We struggle to believe you are good. In the thick of this holy wrestling, we come to you. We pray against the fear of honesty, we pray for courage, and we pray with hope, as we say "if only." According to your goodness and mercies, we pray. Amen.

5 | 📖 JOHN 11:17-45

CHAPTER FIVE

IF ONLY

In October 2014, we faced a terminal diagnosis as a family. The doctors reported that my dad had pancreatic cancer, and it had spread. He had already lost a lot of weight. He could not eat. My brother shaved my dad's head in anticipation of hair loss from the chemotherapy. I took him to his one and only chemotherapy treatment. The cancer was so advanced and aggressive that chemo offered no hope. He never even had a chance to experience that hair loss. "If only" appeared in our family conversations in various ways. If only we had an answer to pancreatic cancer. If only it was not the slow killer. If only we had known about it sooner. If only....

Our living grief was brief as my dad passed away a mere two months later. We buried him two days before Christmas. As I faced losing him to cancer, all I wanted was freedom from the weight of loss and sadness. I was tired of the tossing and turning of the waves of sorrow and the exhaustion of living without him. I had to step into the reality of a different kind of life. I felt completely at the mercy of misery. At times, I wanted to ignore my pain and push through with my hanging-by-a-thread willpower. At other times, I did not want to move, lying comfortably in bed. And then I found an unexpected friend—grief.

Grief was not the friend I was looking for, nor did I welcome her. As I wept and fought anxiety and sleeplessness, I did not want to befriend grief. Yet grief continued to call out to me like a faithful friend. As I drowned in the crashing waves of sorrow, my efforts to manage the sadness failed me. My sadness was merciless, and again, grief reached out her hand, always ready to walk with me. When I finally received grief as a friend, God brought healing through her friendship.

I also found my human friends, those I could text or call anytime and anywhere. They were few, and they were faithful. They listened to my questions, they watched my ugly tears, they gave me space to rest, and they spoke truth at just the right moments. They journeyed along the road of grief with me, and for them I am eternally grateful. To find friends who will walk with you in grief is to find a great treasure.

Loss is no stranger to anyone. We all lose relationships, people, roles, and abilities. We all face loss. Yet grief can be a stranger. We push away grief's invitation of friendship. To embrace deep loss is difficult and heart-wrenching, and it requires more from us than we want to give.

The God of the universe is familiar with loss and grief. Wherever we are in facing loss and wondering what to do with grief, God welcomes us as we are and listens lovingly to our "if onlys."

We find this beautiful truth in the story of two sisters, Martha and Mary. Whether we need to process our pain verbally or sit silently, whether we want to hash things out on our own or dialogue with others, or whether we grow immediately or take a while, God willingly listens and meets us right where we are.

IF ONLY

When we lose something, we often look back to see what we could have changed. What could we have done to bring about a different result? How could we have changed our actions or our words? If we had waited one more minute, how would the present be different? In our "if onlys," we restlessly wonder why God did not allow a different outcome.

"If only" can be a curiosity question, wondering about a different outcome. Often it is much deeper than that. We are looking for someone or something to blame. We need an answer to the why of our pain.

Two sisters, Mary and Martha, had their "if only" moment with the death of their brother, Lazarus. Mary and Martha both directed their "if only" questions to Jesus.

ⓜ PRACTICE

Read John 11:17–32. As you read the passage, focus on verses 21 and 32. Notice the way the sisters approached Jesus with their "if onlys." Have you found yourself using the words "if only" or similar language as you replay scenarios of loss in your mind? What are the regular circumstances you replay in order to change the results?

_____

_____

_____

_____

_____

_____

_____

_____

_____

_____

_____

_____

_____

_____

🎙 PRAYER

Reflect on your "if onlys." Ask God to show you your deeper heart's desire when you think, "If only." Offer these deep desires to God in prayer. Ask him to help you grow in trusting him with your innermost yearnings.

God, if only . . .

_____

_____

_____

_____

_____

_____

_____

_____

_____

_____

_____

GO THERE

Direct communication is scarce. More than likely, you will find someone cautious to speak their mind, ignoring the other person or expressing their disappointment in a passive-aggressive way. We need courage when sharing our disappointments with another. And the courage to go there with the other person gives way for authentic conversation and deeper levels of relationship.

It took great courage for these two sisters to share honestly with Jesus. Yet they did just that. They knew Jesus well enough to speak directly to him.

🕍 PRACTICE

Read John 11:20–32. What do you notice about the sisters' approach to Jesus? What did they express?

What do you do with your thoughts and feelings when you have been let down? Do you talk to the person? Do you run from conversation and potential conflict? Do you bottle it up?

How about with God? Do you pray authentically about your disappointments? If yes, how so? If not, what do you hold back and why?

_____

_____

_____

_____

_____

_____

_____

_____

_____

_____

_____

_____

_____

🎤 PRAYER

Reflecting on your answers above, how do you want to grow in your communication with God? Do you need courage? Do you need trust? Ask God to show you how you need to grow in prayer. Write a prayer expressing any resistance to go there with God, and ask him to assure you that you can go there in honesty with your disappointments.

_____

_____

_____

_____

_____

_____

_____

_____

_____

_____

_____

TRUTH AND TEARS

No two people are the same. In any life circumstance, two people will respond differently. One person wants to talk about it, seeking understanding through knowledge. Another person needs to be quiet, internally processing the incident. Others need to do something—anything.

God knows we are different. He created us uniquely. Our experiences, personalities, birth orders, temperaments, pain, passions, and other factors have shaped us and contribute to how we respond to life's circumstances. Martha and Mary, two sisters, interacted very differently with Jesus as they processed the pain of losing their brother. Jesus welcomed them both.

🕍 **PRACTICE**

Read John 11:20–32. Notice how Martha engaged Jesus and how Jesus responded to her. Observe how Mary spoke to Jesus and how Jesus answered her. Do you identify with one sister more than the other? What do you notice about Jesus's response to each sister? What does this tell you about who Jesus is? What expectations does he have of you in your grieving?

_____

_____

_____

_____

_____

_____

🎙 PRAYER

Do you believe Jesus would respond to you wherever you are, even as he did with the two sisters? If you have hesitations, tell him about them. If you have confidence, thank him for it. Spend time in prayer asking God to deepen your faith where you are.

_____

_____

_____

_____

_____

_____

_____

_____

_____

_____

JOINING OUR GRIEF

Grief is incredibly sacred, and to be invited to share someone's grief is a privilege. There are so many different ways to join in someone's grief—listening to stories, providing thoughtful gifts or words, offering a sounding board for anger, or sitting in the quietness of flowing tears. The invitation to grieve with another can come from someone close to us or a stranger. And sometimes we don't know what to do.

Jesus joined Mary in her grief. He joined her in her tears, even though he knew he had the power to take away her grief. He chose to honor her sorrow and met her in it.

🕋 PRACTICE

Read John 11:33–37. List Jesus's actions in these verses. What do they tell you about Jesus's character? What do you feel as you watch this interaction between Jesus, Mary, and her community? Imagine what it would be like for Jesus to respond to you the same way as you face deep loss. What does imagining this bring up to you?

_____

_____

_____

_____

_____

_____

_____

_____

_____

_____

_____

_____

_____

_____

🎙 PRAYER

Take some time to be honest with God about your tears. What do you think of them? What do they represent to you? Are they something to be hidden or something to share? Ask God to show you what you believe about the vulnerability of tears. If your thoughts about crying need to change, ask God to help you see tears as he wants you to see them.

_____

_____

_____

_____

_____

_____

_____

_____

_____

_____

_____

HOLY ANGER

Death is never a gift. It may be a mercy to die, but death is never a gift. God only gives good gifts, and life is a good gift. God hates death and is greatly angered by it. He longs to make all things new when death will be no more. One day, he will make all things new.

As Jesus interacted with the sisters and their friends, his anger welled up within him, and he was deeply moved and troubled. Some Bible translations capture the depth to which Jesus was angered by death. Others soften it a bit. In this moment, he raged with holy anger at the devastation caused by death, and he wept with his friends.

⦿ PRACTICE

Read John 11:33, 38. What do you think of anger? Must we always keep it under control? Can it be unleashed? How can the anger of Jesus free you to express your anger at death, pain, and loss?

_____

_____

_____

_____

_____

_____

_____

_____

_____

_____

_____

_____

_____

🎙 PRAYER

Talk to God today about your thoughts on anger. Maybe you need to confess damaging anger. Maybe you need to be honest about your anger. Maybe you need to get angry about the things that anger God. Spend time writing a prayer about the emotion of anger and how God wants you to grow in understanding and expressing it.

_____

_____

_____

_____

_____

_____

_____

_____

_____

_____

_____

_____

COMMUNITY

Loss leaves us vulnerable. In our vulnerability, we want to hide. Desiring to maintain an image of strength, we put on a fake smile and hide when we hurt. We do not let just anyone into our pain. When our wounds fester, we take cover, protecting ourselves from anyone who will exacerbate our pain.

Martha and Mary had an incredible community who stayed by their sides in their grief, a community who wept with them. This is so very different from the culture and expectations to which we are accustomed.

PRACTICE

Read John 11:17–37. This time, notice the actions of the community. Notice the role of the community. Has there been a time when you felt alone in your suffering and longed for people to walk with you? Has there been a time when you had the opportunity to join someone's suffering and you ignored their pain because it was too awkward? Write down any experiences of a faithful community as well as an absence of community.

_____

_____

_____

_____

_____

_____

_____

_____

_____

_____

_____

🎙 PRAYER

Pray this prayer today, adding anything you need to include:

Thank you, Jesus, for seeing, for engaging, and for entering our world. You grieved just as Martha and Mary did. And you join us in our grief. Would you give us the attentiveness to notice when others in our lives grieve? Would you help us pause and give us compassion and the wisdom to listen? Would you prepare us for whoever you want to bring our way? Would you help us love others as you did? It is in your loving name we pray. Amen.

_____

_____

_____

_____

_____

_____

_____

_____

_____

_____

_____

_____

LIFE AGAIN

God brings life from death. From the very beginning of creation, he has been and will forever be a life-giver. As God brings life from death, he shows us his great power over death. Death does not and will not have the final word. God is stronger.

Through the sisters' pain, God gave their community new life and new faith. As the story of Lazarus and the sisters ends, the story of people in the community begins. He brings life from death. Only God could do that.

🕍 **PRACTICE**

Read John 11:38–45. As you read this portion of the story, put yourself in the shoes of the community who grieved right along with Mary and Martha. These friends had walked with the sisters in their grief since Lazarus died. Jesus's display of power brought many people to spiritual life as they believed.

Spiritually speaking, what do you believe about God's power to bring life from death? Have you seen him do this? When and how? Write down the story.

_____

_____

_____

_____

_____

_____

_____

_____

_____

_____

_____

🎤 PRAYER

Spend time praising God for the ways you have seen him bring life from death. Sit in the wonder of it for a moment.

Ask God how he wants to use your stories of new life to bring new life to others. Write a prayer of faith, asking God to make your life a display of God's power. Ask him to give you the courage to share these stories so others will experience life.

_____

_____

_____

_____

_____

_____

_____

_____

_____

_____

_____

_____

OPENING **PRAYER**

Loving God, sometimes we are done. We work long and hard, and we feel weary. We are overlooked and unappreciated. And in such moments, we want to give up. Maybe it is time to give up. Or is it time to keep going? Often, we don't know. In these times of weariness, speak to us and tell us where we need to rely on you. Remind us of your care and that you see our struggles. Give us strength, and speak hope into our hearts. May we always be willing to hear from you and receive whatever you have for us as you call us to live and love. Amen.

6 | 📕 1 KINGS 19:1-8

CHAPTER SIX
ENOUGH

Overlooked, underestimated, and misunderstood, I was tired. Exhausted from having to prove myself in a man's world, I was done. Weariness worked its way down to my soul. "Enough, already!" I told God. I wrestled with my call; I wondered if there was something else to pursue. I wanted to be seen. I wept and doubted on more than one occasion. In one tearful conversation, when I expressed my thoughts and feelings to a friend, he reminded me of the time the prophet Elijah told God, "Enough!"

My friend reminded me that God still provided, that God did not forget me, and that I was not the only one God called to serve in this environment. It did not necessarily answer my question of whether to go or whether to stay. Elijah's story did remind me that God sees, provides, and gives life and that he comes with a gentler perspective than we do.

When have you said "I am done" to God? Whether it was with your mouth, your head, your heart, or your body, when have you said, "Enough"?
We may not need to speak the words, but everything about us communicates that we are done. We withdraw, we shut down, we ignore, we pretend, and we are poised to move on.

Elijah served God with tenacity. He spoke for God, he went to battle for God, and he performed miracles in God's name. We would describe him as a success. Yet after one of his greatest successes, he was ready to call it quits. "Enough!" he told God. In loneliness, despair, and exhaustion, he was done.

God heard Elijah's words as well as his heart. God hears you as well.

God saw Elijah, and God wanted Elijah to see him. God wants you to see him as well.

CATCHING YOUR BREATH

Experiencing a victory you never thought would come can be oh so satisfying. Yet all the blood, sweat, and tears can leave you weary. In the midst of bone-dry weariness, the emotions of elation cannot carry you through to your next challenge. All you want is time to catch your breath. Will it come?

In today's reading, Elijah has come off of a recent triumph—a big one. Instead of running a victory lap, he ran for his life. Jezebel, the wicked queen in power, was livid about Elijah's success and hell-bent to murder him. Elijah ran.

🛐 PRACTICE

Read 1 Kings 19:1–3. Consider Elijah's initial response of fear to Jezebel's threat. Has fear ever crept into your heart immediately after a success? How about doubt? When has fear or doubt led you to keep running rather than find rest?

_____

_____

_____

_____

_____

_____

_____

_____

_____

_____

_____

_____

_____

_____

🎙 PRAYER

Take the words you wrote down and make them a prayer to God. Share out loud with God your fears and doubts that have led you to run rather than rest. Ask him to help you rest in him. Pray as you are, with complete transparency, knowing that God loves you.

_____

_____

_____

_____

_____

_____

_____

_____

_____

_____

_____

ALONE

Fear brings isolation, constructing strong, protective walls around us. Even in the presence of others, we can still feel utterly alone. Our tendency to move away from people leads to deeper isolation with our hearts, minds, and bodies tumbling into a spiral of despair. It takes courage to remain in relationships. Elijah had one companion with him as he ran. But Elijah left him behind, choosing instead to be alone.

🏛 PRACTICE

Read 1 Kings 19:3–4. Observe Elijah's actions before he collapsed in exhaustion and despair. Ask God to show you the significance of Elijah running and leaving someone behind. Why do you think Elijah went into the wilderness? Spend time reflecting on a time when you ran away from others and moved into a deeper wilderness of isolation. Write about that time.

_____

_____

_____

_____

_____

_____

_____

_____

_____

_____

_____

_____

_____

🎙 PRAYER

Write or speak a prayer based on the reflections of your lonely, wilderness time. Express your thoughts, emotions, and painful memories to God. Ask God to show you how he was there with you and at work in your life. Ask God to show you what he wants you to learn from this new picture of the wilderness where he was with you.

_____

_____

_____

_____

_____

_____

_____

_____

_____

_____

_____

_____

_____

ENOUGH

Sometimes life is too much. We feel overwhelmed by budgets and bills, children and education, loss and persevering. We spin plates at work, trying to keep bosses happy, clients satisfied, and ourselves content. Our parents are ailing, and we have a strained relationship with our siblings. When the pressure of stress bears down, we want to say, with Elijah, "Enough! I'm done!" Elijah had been serving God, winning battles for him and taking down the bad guys. Suddenly, one bad guy comes after Elijah, and he calls it quits.

🏛 PRACTICE

Read 1 Kings 19:3–4. Have you ever felt so burned out that all you wanted to do was catch your breath? Your mind spins, your body feels frenzied, and your heart has nothing to give. Have you ever said, "Enough! I am done"? Describe this time.

_____

_____

_____

_____

_____

_____

_____

_____

_____

_____

_____

_____

_____

🎙 PRAYER

As you reflect on your experience of exhaustion, write down an honest prayer to God. Tell him about your weariness, your weakness, your longing to truly rest. Be transparent before him and fight the temptation to hide your weakness and muster up your own strength. This prayer will take brutal honesty. Take your time to write it.

_____

_____

_____

_____

_____

_____

_____

_____

_____

_____

_____

ESCAPE

We all have our escapes. For some, it is food. For others, it is drink. Some of us spend money, while others travel to escape. Getaways from the pressures of life can be healthy and life-giving. Escapes can also reveal a desire to deny reality and ignore stressful situations. Our escapes often represent opportunities to surrender to God's grace and strength. Often, however, our attempts to run away reveal our desire to maintain control instead of trusting God to provide the strength we need.

Elijah decided to run and avoid his reality. When he stopped, he nestled under the shade of a tree and slept.

🏮 PRACTICE

Read 1 Kings 19:5a. Where do you run when you feel overwhelmed? How about when you are frustrated? What do you do to ignore the reality of pain in your life? Write these things down. This is an observation exercise. Take any thoughts of shame, embarrassment, or beating yourself up to the Lord in prayer.

_____

_____

_____

_____

_____

_____

_____

_____

_____

_____

_____

_____

🎙 PRAYER

Spend time writing a prayer of surrender, acknowledging that you turn to your escapes instead of to God. Confess to him how you run from his call for you rather than running to him in prayer. As you write this prayer of surrender, remember that God wants to provide all you need to accomplish his call on your life, including forgiveness.

God, I confess ...

_____

_____

_____

_____

_____

_____

_____

_____

_____

_____

_____

_____

PROVISION

God's strength and provision can come in unexpected ways. Whether you receive a word of encouragement, an unexpected meal, or the gift of rest, God provides. He sees us and longs to give us what we need. And through this provision, he empowers us to do what he asks.

For Elijah, an unexpected visitor came with a much-needed provision.

🏮 PRACTICE

Read 1 Kings 19:5–6. Who initiated the provision in the story of Elijah? Does that give you any encouragement? How so?

Take time to remember when God provided for you in unexpected ways. How did his provision strengthen you?

_____

_____

_____

_____

_____

_____

_____

_____

_____

_____

_____

_____

_____

🎙 PRAYER

In what ways do you need God's strength for your journey? Write a prayer about your journey, asking God for what you need. Since we do not always know what we need, ask for the ability to recognize his provision. With a posture of receptivity and gratitude, keep a lookout for God's provision. You never know who or what will show up.

_____

_____

_____

_____

_____

_____

_____

_____

_____

_____

_____

_____

_____

CHOOSING TO CONTINUE

Elijah called it quits, but God was calling him to continue. God knew what he had planned for Elijah and what he needed to continue the journey. God's angel told Elijah that the journey would be too great for him. Again, God provided the physical sustenance Elijah needed and gave him strength for the journey. Elijah still had to choose to receive his provision and fulfill God's call. In the end, Elijah chose to receive and chose to continue.

🕌 **PRACTICE**

Read 1 Kings 19:7–8. When you feel overwhelmed by a path God has called you to walk, how do you typically respond? Are there recurring thought patterns? If so, describe and write them down.

_____

_____

_____

_____

_____

Write about the provisions of strength God has given you throughout your life. What happened when you received God's gift of strength?

_____

_____

_____

_____

_____

_____

What would it look like to recognize your weakness and receive his provision?

_____

_____

_____

_____

_____

🎤 PRAYER

Talk to God in prayer about your thought patterns when you feel overwhelmed. Ask him to provide ways for you to address any negative thought patterns. Ask him to help you receive his gift of strength in your weakness. Express any doubts or questions you have about whether his power and grace will really be enough. Pray for the faith and courage to trust him as he provides.

_____

_____

_____

_____

_____

_____

THE RESPONSE OF GRACE

Elijah's story does not end here. His story goes on to show us God's unexpected gift of grace. God heard Elijah's cry but never granted his desperate request. In fact, God granted something only one other person ever experienced. Elijah never died.

Elijah felt so overwhelmed that the only way he saw out of his difficulty was through death. Yet God was ready to provide another way out, a way that required complete dependence on him. God also provided a companion and successor, Elisha, who never left Elijah's side. And then, in God's great grace, Elijah never experienced death. As God called Elijah to continue, God provided him strength and friendship and then graciously ushered Elijah from the earth.

🏠 PRACTICE

Read 2 Kings 2:1–11. As you read further in Elijah's story, what truths about God fill your mind? In knowing Elijah's story, what will you believe about God? Write these things down. Spend time today meditating on these truths of who God is.

_____

_____

_____

_____

_____

_____

_____

_____

_____

_____

_____

_____

🎤 PRAYER

Write a prayer of praise to God, thanking him for his love, grace, and provision. Be honest with him about your struggle to believe as well as your hopes of deeper faith. In this prayer, ask God to show ways he provided for you, reminding you of his goodness. Ask him to help you trust that he will continue to provide for you in the days to come.

_____

_____

_____

_____

_____

_____

_____

_____

_____

_____

_____

OPENING **PRAYER**

Faithful Father, how often we look for you in the extraordinary and on the mountaintop. We long to catch glimpses of you in special places and moments. But often, we don't expect you in the ordinary. Yet the ordinary is where we live most of the time, and you promise to meet us there. As we live our everyday lives, open our eyes to see you. Help us see that in the everyday routines of life, you offer beautiful gifts just for us. In great expectancy, we pray. Amen.

CHAPTER SEVEN
GIVE ME

When it is time to meet with God, I drive to a café near our home, find a booth that looks out a window, and drink hot tea—not coffee, hot tea. Hot tea slows me down. And it's not any café; it's this one. It's quieter. It's not just any booth; it's a booth near a window. The wide-open space (even though it overlooks a parking lot) is good for my soul. As we sit together, I wait for him to show me the root of my wrestling. As he reminds me of his truth, it sinks deeper. There is nothing particularly magical about meeting God in this café, in this booth by a window, with a cup of tea. Yet he repeatedly meets me in this space, atmosphere, and light. However, to believe he only comes to this particular place and space would be so limiting.

God comes to us in the everyday places and spaces. He comes to us in the dark, in the light, in the hidden, and in the open. God comes. And the thing is, he is always the one who comes first. He initiates the conversation.

For a Samaritan woman, Jesus came to her on a normal day, during a routine task. She was getting water. Jesus needed water. Pretty basic. Yet this interaction, initiated by Jesus, led to a transformational conversation. This woman thirsted for what Jesus had to offer, but she did not know it. It took time and banter, curiosity and dialogue, to see the gift of life Jesus had for her.

EVERYDAY PLACES

Ordinary is not exciting. Familiar tasks often turn into monotonous, dull requirements. There is nothing to look forward to when doing the basics. In the ordinary, our minds wander to other more mesmerizing experiences and daring dreams. We might even find ourselves grumbling about the ordinary. When it comes to prayer, we often ask for and imagine things that can be, with anticipation that they will be. And then to live in the ordinary seems like such a letdown.

Yet Jesus comes to us in the drab, commonplace tasks of life. For the Samaritan woman, he came in the ordinary task of fetching water. In this ordinary task, Jesus initiated an extraordinary conversation.

🛆 PRACTICE

Read John 4:1–7. As you read the beginning of this story, think about the mundane things in your life. Write a list of the things you do every day that seem plain and ordinary.

_____

_____

_____

_____

_____

_____

_____

_____

_____

_____

_____

_____

_____

🎤 PRAYER

Look over your list and pick one or two of the tasks. Write a prayer asking God to meet you in these ordinary tasks. Maybe he wants you to offer gratitude during that task, or maybe that task reminds you of someone to pray for or call. Write a prayer, listen to God, and act on what he asks you to do.

_____

_____

_____

_____

_____

_____

_____

_____

_____

_____

GIVE ME

The pursuit of the extraordinary is a high value in our American culture. We celebrate and compensate the exceptional. We go hard and fast after anything but the mundane. But the ordinary times in life slow us down and give us the opportunity to breathe. As we slow down, we see our need for God and move into a deeper relationship with him. Repeated routines can frustrate us, or they can help us dig deeply. As the ordinary exposes the reality of our humanity and capacities, there is opportunity for our true worth to be recognized.

The Samaritan woman was in the midst of an ordinary task with an ordinary outcome. Yet Jesus was about to meet her with an extraordinary gift. They conversed over the subject of water, a simple need and one deeper than she realized.

🖤 PRACTICE

Read John 4:8–15. In this interaction of Jesus and the woman, what stands out to you about the Samaritan woman? What stands out to you about Jesus? If God were to interact with you over something ordinary, what would it be? Where does he want you to slow down so he can talk with you?

_____

_____

_____

_____

_____

_____

_____

_____

_____

_____

_____

_____

🎙 PRAYER

Take a deep breath today and slow down. Sit with God over a cup of hot tea or go on a long, slow walk. Talk with him while folding laundry or driving to the office. Turn off the music and sit in silence. Spend 15 minutes with him in quiet prayer, asking him a simple "meet me, show me, give me what I need from you today."

_____

_____

_____

_____

_____

_____

_____

_____

_____

_____

FROM DIALOGUE TO DEPTH

Jesus knows and goes to places we might not be ready for. What we believe is a safe conversation with Jesus often pushes us deeper into the places in our heart and mind than we are prepared to go. Our responses vary from welcome to walls, from increased dialogue to silence, from tears to questions. When God meets us, he moves us. Encountering God demands that we change. How we respond is up to us.

Jesus met the woman with a truth she never revealed to him. As he did, she engaged him. She went into a theological banter with him about worship, about her people, about truth. And as she sought truth, she found it.

(🕯) **PRACTICE**

Read John 4:16–26. Is there a moment or a pain that has shaped you more than you would like? Have you allowed him to meet you in that moment or that pain? How about the aftereffects? Spend time today with Jesus in that moment or pain. Whatever it is, allow God to speak to you through banter, questions, and depth. Engage him in conversation and prayer.

_____

_____

_____

_____

_____

_____

_____

_____

_____

_____

_____

_____

_____

🎙 PRAYER

Write down prayers that have come from your practice today. Ask God to continue to show you what he has to offer you, just as he offered the woman the living water of salvation. Ask him for reminders of his love for you.

_____

_____

_____

_____

_____

_____

_____

_____

_____

_____

MORE THAN WE IMAGINED

God's grace is far greater and richer than we can imagine. In his goodness, he comes to us in the ordinary, inviting us to talk with him. He has unlimited and undistracted time for us. His grace works beyond our questions and doubts, straight to our longings. His grace cuts through our resistance to give us life.

Jesus graciously initiated, engaged, and interacted with the Samaritan woman. He met her in the ordinary and gave her space to voice her questions. His interaction also gave her hope that he had what she desperately needed— living water.

PRACTICE

Read John 4:1–26. Ask God to show you what you desperately need. Maybe you need the living water of salvation. Maybe you need to admit that you have needs. Maybe you need to rest in his provision and satisfaction for your soul. Ask God what you need and write down what he reveals. Watch for his provision in the coming moments, days, and months.

_____

_____

_____

_____

_____

_____

_____

_____

_____

_____

_____

_____

🎙 PRAYER

Our needs are not always met in our timing, and that can be discouraging. We wonder if God sees us or hears us. Write a prayer of honesty. Offer your real thoughts and emotions as questions flood your mind. Surrender to him, trusting that he will satisfy your deepest longings. Even if it is difficult, end with an offer of gratitude for his grace, knowing that his grace is sufficient.

_____

_____

_____

_____

_____

_____

_____

_____

_____

_____

_____

_____

COME, SEE

Our stories are God's stories. His transformation in our lives is a gift to us and a gift to others. We are the only ones who can truly tell our stories. We have the privilege to share God's grace in our lives and point others to our God who is able to do great things.

The woman in the story encountered a great God and told others to come and see. Her brief interaction, in an ordinary place, led to an extraordinary realization that maybe this was the one they had been waiting for—the Messiah who would save them.

🏠 PRACTICE

Read John 4:27–30. As you read the actions of the woman and the response of the people in town, how do the actions strike you? Are you surprised, confused, excited? How did the woman use her life story and her interaction with Jesus to influence the people she knew?

_____

_____

_____

_____

🎤 PRAYER

Spend time in prayer today asking God what part of your story he wants you to share. Ask him to show you the people he wants you to share it with. Write down your story and a list of the people with whom you want to interact. Write a prayer asking God to give you courage and joy as you share his story in your life. Then go share it.

_____

_____

_____

_____

_____

_____

_____

_____

_____

_____

_____

_____

OUR WORK

Part of the work for those who know Jesus is to notice others who don't know Jesus. When we fill our lives with tasks to accomplish and places to go, we miss the people God has placed in our paths. God calls us to open our eyes, to see, and to move with intent toward those who are waiting to know him. They may not know they need him until you tell them. Through the Holy Spirit, God gives us the sight to see and the courage to move toward them.

Jesus talked to his disciples about the work he set out to do. In fact, he had just done that work as he talked with the Samaritan woman. Jesus does not ask us to do what he did not do. He pursued people in routine tasks of life and shared with them the extraordinary gift of God—salvation.

PRACTICE

Read John 4:31–38. As you read this portion of the story and think about the work Jesus calls his followers to, what thoughts and feelings come to the surface? Do you doubt that people truly need Jesus? Are you afraid of saying the wrong thing? Do you wonder whether it is really up to you to tell people about God? Be honest with yourself and be honest with God.

_____

_____

_____

_____

_____

_____

🎤 PRAYER

Pray this prayer today, adding anything you need to include:

Gracious God, you have given us a good work to do, telling others about Jesus. He is the hope of the world, the one who will make all things new. If there are any fears or doubts about talking about Jesus, would you meet us in them? Help us believe he truly is the greatest gift to anyone. Give us joy, courage, and faith to love and tell others about Jesus. It is in his incredible name we pray. Amen.

FAITH TO FAITH

During a New Year's Day sermon, I shared about God's gift of forgiveness to me regarding my relationship with my mom. A woman in the congregation later came to me and told me about the broken relationship with her dad. She told me that hearing what God did in my life encouraged her to ask God for a miracle in hers. God responded, providing the same freedom and grace for her. I was surprised and overjoyed to share with her in God's goodness. I did not know she had a broken relationship with her dad—her life looked perfect. I didn't know, but God did.

One ordinary moment can lead to many extraordinary moments. From the faith of one woman to the faith of a community, we see what happens when we let God speak to us, meet us, and give us life. This life then spreads to life for others.

Through the interaction in the ordinary, many people came to faith because of this woman. That is the power of our story, of God's story and work in our life. May our stories continue to tell of his great story of love and salvation to everyone we encounter.

PRACTICE

Read John 4:39–42. As you read these verses, make note of the progression of faith that happens in this community. What does it stir in you? What does it make you think about? How does this encourage you? Write down the communities in which you have a voice of influence to share your story.

_____

_____

_____

_____

_____

_____

_____

_____

_____

_____

🎙 PRAYER

Write a prayer for faith. Ask for increased faith for yourself. Ask for faith for the people near you. Ask for courage, ask for love, and ask for grace. Ask for wisdom and joy in pointing people to Jesus, whether in the extraordinary or ordinary. And watch faith crash like a wave, covering the world around you.

_____

_____

_____

_____

_____

_____

_____

_____

_____

_____

OPENING **PRAYER**

Father God, you know our hearts. You know our thoughts. We have expectations, hopes, and dreams. We imagine outcomes that pull us out of circumstances, ease our pain, and give us freedom. We have longings and attempt to believe the impossible. You tell us that you can do the impossible. Yet you don't always choose to do the impossible things we hope for. At those times, we wonder why you don't. When our hopes and dreams are dashed, we lose the courage and resilience to hope again. So, Father, hear our hearts as we attempt to place our hope in you. Hear us in our disappointment and show us the way to hope again. In your mercy and grace, we pray. Amen.

8 | 📖 LUKE 24:13-35

CHAPTER EIGHT

WE HAD HOPED

Lost hope can be devastating. It is one thing to be in the middle of hopeful times, waiting for God to answer our prayers. But it's quite another to be on the other side of waiting, with our hopes and dreams left unfulfilled. When my dad was diagnosed with pancreatic cancer, I had hope that he could fight the cancer. We all did. We would do whatever it took to fight, and we had hope because we lived near the best cancer hospital in the world with the best team of doctors, tailor-fit for my dad. I even wrote him a card, pleading with him to keep fighting. He never had the chance.

I begged God for one more Christmas with my dad. I asked others to pray this prayer with me. He died one week before Christmas, and we buried him on December 23, 2014.

Many of us are familiar with lost hope. The hysterectomy that leads to the lost hope of bearing a child. The silent phone that leads to the lost hope of a job. The death that tells us we will not see or talk to our friend again. When something is hoped for and lost, our hearts take a blow. Our sadness, our disappointment, our confusion overwhelm us. We wait for rescue, and it never comes. What do we do after lost hope?

Two men walked the road of lost hope after Jesus's death. They had hoped Jesus would rescue them from a tyrannical government. They had hoped he would bring salvation for their people. But he didn't. He died. And when Jesus died, their hopes died with him.

As these men literally and figuratively walked this road of confusion and disappointment, they had no idea another person would join them. This person would remind them of God's promises and provide a better hope than they ever dreamed.

MAKING SENSE

When the unexplainable happens, we want to make sense of it. We find ourselves thinking and talking about it, repeatedly. Devastating natural disasters seem to play on the news in an unending loop, echoing stories of loss and pain. A lone gunman rages against innocent victims, reminding us of the swiftness of life and injustices of this world. As we are inundated by updates, we try to make sense of the unexplainable, desperately seeking understanding.

Two men watched the headlines in the city of Jerusalem. An incredible man, believed by some to be the promised Messiah, died a criminal's death. As they talked about it, another man joined them, seemingly unaware of the headlines.

🏛 PRACTICE

Read Luke 24:13–14. Two men walked and talked about their confusion, longing for clarity. How did they choose to engage their circumstances? What can you learn from their actions?

How do you respond in the unexplainable? What do you do when you feel confused, unsure, and struggling to hope? What do you do to make sense of it all?

_____

_____

_____

_____

_____

_____

_____

_____

_____

_____

_____

🎤 PRAYER

Rest in this prayer and repeat it as necessary:

Gracious Father, how we want to make sense of our lives. We want to know why, how, and for what purpose. In our confusion, we seek clarity. In our hopelessness, we escape. In the midst of the insensible, teach us to turn to you. Remind us of your presence with us even though we may not see you. Thank you that you walk with us no matter how dark the path. In Jesus's name, we pray. Amen.

_____

_____

_____

_____

_____

_____

_____

_____

_____

_____

_____

_____

WELCOMING GOD

With lost hope, we respond in various ways. Sometimes, we hold our loss and grief in private, protecting ourselves from additional pain. Sometimes, we courageously let others in, and we choose to welcome God into our broken hearts. We go there with God and take a risk to welcome him into the conversation. We believe it is worth it.

On the road, a stranger entered the scene and began to walk with the men. The men engaged the stranger and yet were kept from seeing who he truly was. Jesus inquired about their conversation, seemingly unaware of the headlines. They stopped in their tracks, with sadness cemented on their faces. He graciously played dumb and let them talk.

🏮 PRACTICE

Read Luke 24:15–20. As you read this portion of the story, is there anything that surprises you or catches you off guard about Jesus's actions? What aspect of this interaction leaves you curious or wondering about God's actions? What disappointments have led you to leave God out of the conversation? When have you courageously engaged him in conversation?

_____

_____

_____

_____

_____

_____

_____

_____

_____

_____

_____

_____

🎙 PRAYER

Sometimes, we are afraid to let God into our pain. We gladly talk to people about our experiences, but not God. Write a prayer about your fears or hesitations about sharing with God your sadness, disappointment, and pain. Confess to him the times you have run to others instead of running to him. Ask him to heal your heart and grow your trust in him so you will run to him first, even if you feel afraid.

_____

_____

_____

_____

_____

_____

_____

_____

_____

_____

_____

COVER UP

Cover it up, ignore it, stuff it, hide it. We are conditioned to hide our sadness, to do anything but admit it and show it. We are to pretend it is not there. Sadness is not an emotion to honor and engage, but an emotion to disregard. It is a nuisance. It does not move us forward and has no power. It is a sign of weakness.

Yet the men on the road with Jesus chose to openly carry the heavy weight of sadness. They did nothing to hide it. When Jesus asked what had happened, they stopped walking and opened up. With sorrow, they retold their story of lost hope.

PRACTICE

Read Luke 24:17. In grief, retelling the story of our pain reminds us that the story is true and not just a nightmare from which we will soon wake up. Retelling our stories of pain is hard. In this passage, Jesus asked the men to retell their story, to give voice to their grief.

How do you respond when someone asks you to repeat a painful story? Do you quickly move on? Do you change the subject? Do you engage the story and relive the pain once again? What do you do with sadness? Write about a time when you chose to open up with your emotions. What happened?

_____

_____

_____

_____

_____

_____

_____

_____

_____

_____

🎤 PRAYER

Take your time writing today. God may need to do a deeper work in you. Talk to him about your positive and negative encounters when you shared your feelings with another. If needed, take a few days on this assignment and ask God to reveal your habits when engaging your own sadness. Ask him about how you respond to another's sadness. Ask him to meet you in these habits and give you the power and practical tools to transform them.

_____

_____

_____

_____

_____

_____

_____

_____

_____

_____

LOST HOPE

Shattered dreams, unmet expectations, unrelenting confusion—the pain is too deep to see a way out, and the fear of disappointment is too strong to fight for another way. Hope looks to the future, but lost hope gets stuck in the past, too paralyzed to move. How do we live in the present with a broken heart?

The men on the road had a companion join them, walk with them, and meet them in their present. They could express their deep disappointments to this companion. In the present, they were honest about their lost hope as well as their uncertainty about the future.

⌂ PRACTICE

Read Luke 24:21. Spend some time reading this verse and imagine how the two men felt. What did they express? Have you ever verbally expressed your feelings of lost hope and unsatisfied expectations? If not, why not? If so, what happened? Do you believe you can be as honest with God as the men on the road were?

_____

_____

_____

_____

_____

_____

_____

_____

_____

_____

_____

_____

🎙 PRAYER

As you reflect on a time in your life when you lost hope, write out a prayer. Express everything you felt at that time. Try to express everything without holding back. As you do, speak your prayer out loud. Maybe you need to go on a run or a walk, take a bath, or just sit still. Whatever will open up the conversation, go do that and talk with God.

_____

_____

_____

_____

_____

_____

_____

_____

_____

_____

_____

_____

CLEARING THE CONFUSION

Truth clears confusion. It is helpful to retrace the facts, look at history, and gather information. During hopelessness and disappointment, it takes discipline to seek the truth and accept it. As you rest in the reality of your painful situation, the confusion will begin to clear, and the fog of misunderstanding will lift.

The two men were obviously confused by Jesus's death. They tried desperately to make sense of their broken expectations. Their travel companion reminded them of God's historical promises that impacted their present reality. With this information came opportunity for a new perspective.

🏛 PRACTICE

Read Luke 24:22–27. Take time today to notice your thought patterns and habits during times of confusion. Do you research to gain more information? Do you crumble with discouragement? Do you isolate or abandon all attempts at understanding? In fogs of confusion, how do you respond and behave?

_____

_____

_____

_____

_____

_____

_____

_____

_____

_____

_____

_____

🎤 PRAYER

Using your observations from your patterns during confusion, talk to God about them. Thank him for creating you the way he did and ask him to show you how you need to respond differently during such times. Ask him to give you the strength to deepen holy habits and spiritual practices of meditating on his truth as you seek understanding.

_____

_____

_____

_____

_____

_____

_____

_____

_____

_____

_____

_____

THE REVELATION

Our human understanding can only take us so far. Our minds are incapable of discerning spiritual realities apart from God's revelation. There comes a point in our conversations with God when we must welcome his revelation. This road of hopelessness and disappointment can be a long one, and in weariness we can give up. At some point, we move beyond receiving truthful information about God to receiving God himself.

The two men already received a lot from their new companion. This unexpected confidante walked with them physically, emotionally, and spiritually. At the end of the day, they were reluctant for him to depart and asked him to join them for food, fellowship, and rest. When their companion welcomed the invitation, he revealed who he was, showing them he was more than a temporary companion but rather the very presence and hope for which they longed.

PRACTICE

Read Luke 24:28–32. As you read this part of the story, notice the actions of the two men and the actions of their walking companion. How did they respond to his revelations?

_____

_____

_____

_____

_____

_____

Write about a time you welcomed Jesus in and he overwhelmed you with his love and goodness. What was that like?

As you reflect on these men and their desire for Jesus to remain with them, consider the times when you have left Jesus at the door—times when exhaustion led you to ignore Jesus's desire to be with you? Is there a place of disappointment and pain into which you can welcome Jesus to sit with you, eat with you, and show himself to you?

_____

_____

_____

_____

_____

🎙 PRAYER

Is there anything you have held back up to this point as we have reflected on the Emmaus story? If so, let it out in prayer. If you are sorry, say it. If you are angry, speak it. If you are tired, moan it. Get it out. Talk to God honestly today. After it's all out, sit quietly and receive your Father's words and his power. He sees you, he loves you, and he makes all things new. And he is ready to show more of himself to you than you could have ever hoped or dreamed.

_____

_____

_____

_____

_____

_____

ROAD OF RETURN

Jesus has been with us all along. He is a faithful companion, teacher, and savior. He gives us what we need at the time we need it. He faithfully walks with us on any and every road. Sometimes Jesus asks us to walk the same road again, but with eyes open and with deeper faith.

The men returned to Jerusalem that same hour, on the same road. But the road had changed because Jesus had changed them. The road of disappointment and hopelessness had become a journey of joy and trust. And when they got back, you'd better believe they told all their friends the story of this faithful Jesus, risen from the dead and walking among them again.

🛐 PRACTICE

Read Luke 24:33–35. The men retraced their steps on a familiar road with fresh eyes and hopeful hearts. It makes you wonder if they replayed in their minds their conversation with Jesus, recognizing his faithfulness every step of the way. Is there a story in your life that you need to retrace and look for God's faithfulness? Has Jesus met you in a new way, and do you have a story to tell others? Is there a story of God's faithfulness that you need to rewalk in order to tell others about Jesus? Spend time considering the roads of return God wants you to recount in order to tell others of his love, goodness, and power. Write these stories down. After you recount them, tell others about them.

_____

_____

_____

_____

_____

_____

_____

_____

_____

_____

_____

🎙 PRAYER

Pray with joy today! Reflect on the stories of God's faithfulness in your life and express your gratitude to Him. Ask him to give you great joy and courage to tell his story to another person. Pray specifically for the person with whom God wants you to share, that they might have ears to hear and eyes to see his story in your life.

_____

_____

_____

_____

_____

_____

_____

_____

_____

_____

_____

EPILOGUE

Our voices matter. Your voice matters, especially to God. He sees your life, knows your heart, and loves you. He is the one who created you. He gave you your voice, and he longs to hear it.

He faithfully initiates and invites you to conversation so you can pour out your heart, your thoughts, your questions, and your curiosities to him. He knows you inside and out, and he patiently listens. He speaks truth and reminds you of his love, kindness, and grace. Would you continue to listen?

My prayer for you is that you would continue talking with God, courageously receiving his love and grace, trusting that he sees and hears you. As you do, may you discover your true voice more deeply as you listen for his. Your voice is found when you talk to the one who created it. Your voice is found when you listen to the one who speaks truth, love, and goodness into your life. Your voice just may surprise you as God moves, heals, and answers both spoken and unspoken prayers. He knows exactly what we need, and he is incredibly good and gracious to give it.

As you continue to pray as you are, may your voice grow in truth, strength, and hope—for you and for the sake of those in this world whom God calls you to love and serve. As God's love surprises you in unimagined ways, may you share your story of his goodness so others may know our good God.

ACKNOWLEDGMENTS

To write a study on prayer without the prayers of others would be impossible. So many have been praying for this project. Their words to God and their words to me have provided the strength, insight, courage, and creativity to write this book.

When it comes to the skills of writing, I never imagined this was my gift. God surprises us all when he weaves our gifts with his strength. I am incredibly grateful to those who pushed me to develop my writing skills.

To my husband, Craig, who champions and challenges me to use my gifts to the fullest, has a word-bank that far surpasses mine, and taught me to befriend the edit feature in Microsoft Word.

To my children, who push me to creativity in so many ways. As I type at our family dinner table (translation: table with Legos, papers, markers, scissors, etc.), I am surrounded by the books they have created—books filled with comic strips, illustrations, and bubble letters.

To my mom, Madlen, who allowed me to share parts of her story. God is always about the work of healing, and he continues to do so for both of us.

To Sandra Glahn, who first told me good writing was about organization of thought and who faithfully walked alongside me.

To Kathy Padgett and Lauren Eastburn, faithful friends, who encouraged me to write to my fullest and offered their edits and encouragements along the way.

To Keith and Megan Peeler, who spoke truth and challenged me to step out in faith rather than dismiss opportunities to receive from others.

To Highland Park Presbyterian Church that gave me the space and resources to develop and discern this gift of writing and took a leap of faith, trusting God would work in and through me for the people of the church and beyond.

To the people in the Puddles Bible study who allowed me to test chapters on them and graciously gave me feedback, encouraged me, and shared their hearts and prayers with me.

To Ann Higginbottom who took time to talk to me about publishing and the call of writing.

To Malia Rodriguez, my editor, who enhanced, clarified, and sharpened my words and thoughts.

To Madalyn Basse, my designer, who listened to the babbling desires for my books, heard them, and then beautifully translated them through illustration and design.

To Lucid Books for the freedom, advice, structure, and team with which to work. Being an author can be incredibly lonely, and I am grateful for this partnership.

To write is to be vulnerable, in more ways than expected. I am grateful for the family and friends who encouraged and championed me to use my voice, to step more deeply into my gifts, and to not be afraid to ask for help along the way.

I am thankful for Leslie Melson, Kathleen Hodges, Martha Hooper, Sheri Onishi, Laurie Connell, Erin Walsh, Sharifa Stevens, Terri Moore, Heather Goodman, Dipa Hart, Charles and Laura Clift, Glenn and Janice Kreider, Reid Slaughter, Teresa Murray, Erin Hicks, Katie Reading, Alisha Pearson, Kelsey Phillips, Andy and Jean Raub, Gail Seidel, Ali Dunagan, Emily Scates, Katie Woodley, Hope Heathcott, Sterling White, Sharon Johnson, Tara Bready, Dede McFarland, and anyone I have forgotten (I am so sorry!).

Most importantly, I am incredibly grateful to our gracious, good, and faithful God who welcomes conversation at any point and place in time. In fact, he is starting another one....